Riddling Rhymes

Riddling Rhymes

DELPHINE EVANS

Illustrated by Shelagh McGee

Beaver Books

A Beaver Book
Published by Arrow Books Limited
62-5 Chandos Place, London WC2N 4NW
An imprint of Century Hutchinson Ltd

London Melbourne Sydney Auckland
Johannesburg and agencies throughout the world

First published in 1988 by Hutchinson Children's Books
under the title *The Really Original Riddle Book*

Beaver edition 1989

Text © Delphine Evans 1988
Illustrations © Shelagh McGee 1988

Set in Plantin by Book Ens, Saffron Walden, Essex

Made and printed in Great Britain
by Courier International Ltd
Tiptree, Essex

ISBN 0 09 961130 9

Contents

Introduction

This book was written because of the great interest shown by children and adults in the few rhyming riddles included in my other books.

All over the country, whenever I meet people, I can guarantee that using these, we are certain to have a great deal of fun! Try them and see!

Rhyming riddles can be used in many different ways:

- Use them *on your own* – just to see how clever you are!
- Use them *with a friend* and take it in turns to ask one another.
- Use them *in groups* – in schools – Brownies – Cubs etc. The easy ones can even be used in Nursery classes and Playgroups. One person (or the teacher/leader) reads the rhyme slowly and those listening see who can answer first!
- Use them *at parties* – as 'listen and think' games, either played as above 'mentally' or as a pen/pencil game and see who wins.
- Use them any time – just when you feel like having a bit of fun!

> I love to write a rhyme
> Whenever I have time.
> These are riddles too
> All for you to do!

All Kinds of Everything

Autumn

1   Green in summer on a tree so tall,
Brown in autumn, to the ground they fall.

2   First I'm a flower with prickles protecting me.
I turn green – red – then black, and I'm very
juicy!

3   I grow on a tree and in hedges as well.
Eat my inside and not my hard shell.

4   In autumn I'm put in a box to sleep.
I stay until spring without even a peep.

Guess who?

5 Dancing, dancing on her toes,
Round and round and round she goes.
Dancing, dancing, all the day,
To tinkling music bright and gay,
She whirls and twirls, she never stops –
The . . . on the . . . . . .

Answer: Dancer on the musical box

What grows?

6 Green and hard and round,
Plant it in the ground.
Sprinkle it with rain.
Then summer's here again.
Every day the acorn's growing,
Oh so gradually.
Times goes by, until at last we see,
It's grown into a big . . . . . .

Answer: Oak tree

What day?

7 A special day comes once a year.
It makes me happy when it's here.
Cards and presents are sent to me –
There's cake and jelly for my tea.
My friends all come, and then we play.
Now, have you guessed?
It's my . . .

Answer: Birthday

Time rhyme

8 I know one clock that makes a noise,
And wakes up sleepy girls and boys.
It's not a watch you only hear
If you press it close against your ear.
It's not the clock up on the wall
That doesn't make a noise at all,
Nor is it Grandfather clock
With its slow tick tock.
No, the one I mean is an .. ...

Who are they?

9   See some little babies
Standing in a row.
See some little babies,
That never ever grow.
They will never walk
On their tiny feet.
For they are ... ...
That we like to eat!

Things to eat

10 This tastes very cold
When you are hot.
It's sweet and it's creamy,
You'll like it a lot.

11 Elephants like them
At the zoo.
They can have cream inside
Or a currant or two!

12 The name of this food
Starts off in the sea.
The end's on your hands
And they're tasty for tea.

Answers: **10** Ice cream, **11** Buns, **12** Fish fingers

16

13 You can put it in coffee,
    You can put it in tea.
    If we didn't have any,
    – How sour we would be!

14 Sometimes it's sliced,
    Sometimes it's not.
    You can't have a sandwich
    If this is forgot!

Answers: **13** Sugar, **14** Bread

Blinking Traffic

15 I wink and I blink
By day and by night,
And people all say,
'What a blinking sight!'

My yellow head's high
On a pole black and white,
And it winks and it blinks
By day and by night.

I stand all day
With a crossing at my feet.
Come and see me
If you need to cross the street.

There are zig-zig lines
For all the cars to see.
Zig zig, zig zag
Nearly touching me.

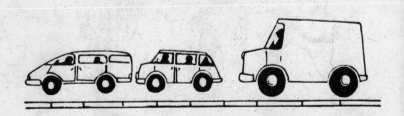

Travel

16 Stops at the station, lets folk get on.
A whistle blows and it's off again.
Away down the track, oh where has it gone?
'Next station, of course,' says the ... ...

17 With the folk snug inside, the engines roar.
It's flying off to some distant shore.
So far, so far, so very high?
It is an ... in the sky.

What are they?

18   'Come with me,' my mother said, 'we'll
      pick a few lambs' tails.
We shall find them as we walk through
      woods and fields and dales.'
I really felt quite worried as I watched
      lambs skiping by.
'Pick their tails?' I said to Mum. 'But
      surely they would cry?'
My mum looked puzzled for a while,
Then smiled a great big smile.
'Not real lambs' tails,' she said to me,
'Look at that lovely hazel tree.
The . . . hanging from each bough
Are called lambs' tails. Let's pick some
      now.'

Who are they?

19   I could see them swimming
Far out on the water,
Mother swimming with her sons
And perhaps her daughter.
I watched them paddling round and round,
Then suddenly they all went down.
I gave a shout, I gave a call,
But there was nothing wrong at all.
For up came one, two, three, four, five
Looking very much alive.
And I realized with shame,
Diving down was just their game.
If I was one I'd do it too.
I'd like to disappear from view.
What did I see?

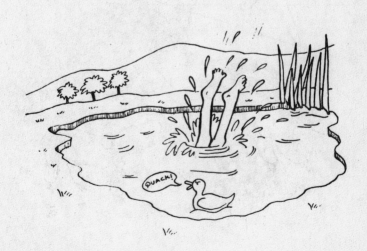

Answer: Ducks

My outing

20 I am going somewhere –
What will I see?
Animals and people, performing for me.
I'll see a man on a high wire, balancing with
   ease,
Dancing horses, a funny clown,
And a girl on a swinging trapeze.
Where am I going?

Chestnut tree

21   Chestnut tree standing tall,
      Growing on a hill.
    Find its fruit, string it through,
      Hold it very still.
    See it dangle, round and shiny,
      Hanging on its string
    Ready, steady, try to hit it,
      If not, I am king!

What is the fruit?

Answer: Conker

Who am I?

22 I'm a happy fellow
With a handle and a spout.
'Have a nice cup of tea,'
You can hear me shout.
The tea leaves tickle me inside
As they swirl about.
See me smiling broadly
As the tea's poured out!

23 Little bird in the garden
Hopping up and down.
Little bird, so pretty.
Coloured red and brown?

Alphabet

Ask anyone

A's the first letter, it comes after no other.
Ask almost anyone, your aunt or your mother
A is for apple and apes in a zoo.
For April and August and autumn too.
For Australia and Africa across the wide sea,
A's always around I think you'll agree.

How many *words* beginning with A or a are in
this rhyme?

B Clever!

B can be before, beside or behind another.
For Bob, Ben, Bert and Bill and also baby brother.
B is for buns, bread and butter for tea
And the buzz-buzz-buzz of the bumble bee!
For bat and for ball and the bird in the nest.
It's true, I believe the B is the best.

How many *words* beginning with B or b are in this rhyme?

C the Cs?

C is for circus and Coco the clown,
For a cosy cup of coffee in a café in the town.
For Christmas carols too on a cold crisp day,
For a cow and her calf, and chickens that lay.
For cliffs to climb over and caves by the coast.
Choose C and maybe you can use it the most!

How many *words* beginning with C or c are in this rhyme?

Answer: 20

27

Do do it!

D is for dates in Dad's diary each day.
For Dachshunds, Dalmatian and donkeys that bray.
For a digger excavating a deep dirty ditch,
A dangerous driver, a dreadful old witch.
For daffodil, dahlia and dandelion tea.
It's not difficult to discover the Ds you will see.

How many *words* beginning with D or d are in this rhyme?

Eesee!

E is for everyone, either English or Eskimo,
Each eye and each ear and even each elbow.
For Elizabeth, Edna and Ernest and Evan,
Who enjoy eating eggs and eclairs at eleven.
For emu and eagle and an e-normous elephant,
Finding E words is easy, exciting and elegant.

How many *words* beginning with E or e are in
this rhyme?

Answer: 27

Fun!

F is for food and fine festive fare,
For feathers on falcons that fly in the air.
For fawns in the field and foals on the farm,
For flickering flames in a fire bright and warm.
For father and football – his favourite game,
For fun with your friends – four or five you could
    name.

How many *words* beginning with F or f are in
this rhyme?

Go for G

G is for gold that glitters and glows
For gondola, galleon and a great gale that blows.
Gardenia, geranium, in gardens they grow.
For giraffe and gazelle as graceful they go.
For a goat who grazes on a grassy green mound,
Play a game – go on, count the Gs you have found.

How many *words* beginning with G or g are in this rhyme?

H'ard or not?

H is for hamster, horse, hare and hedgehog,
Hippopotamus, husky and also hound dog.
For haddock and halibut, herring and hake,
And a hawk hovering high over heather and lake.
For holly and hawthorn with berries bright red,
It's for hat or for helmet to cover your head.

How many *words* beginning with H or h are in
this rhyme?

Interesting?

I is for interesting insects on an island.
Imagine the instruments found in a band.
For Israel, Italy, India too,
And Ireland, and Iceland, and in an igloo.
Ice cream and iceberg I think I'll just mention,
And ideas are important and so is invention.

How many *words* beginning with I or i are in
this rhyme?

Answer: 20

33

Just J

J is for journey in a jeep or a jet
To the jungle where jackals and jaguars are met.
Jill is a journalist, her job is the news,
Jim is a jeweller who has jewels you can choose.
John is a judge and Joe is a jockey,
Jess just likes jigsaws and jazzbands and hockey.

How many *words* beginning with J or j are in
this rhyme?

34

Krazy K

K's for King Kenneth and his knock-kneed knight.
The King keeps a kestrel and flies a kite.
The knock-kneed knight is named Sir Kit.
The Kitchen kettle has a knob that doesn't fit.
The King likes cold kippers which he eats with a
  knife,
The knight prefers kedgeree cooked by his wife.

How many *words* beginning with K or k are in
this rhyme?

Answer: 21

Look for L

L's for large lions and leopards that leap,
For a lost lamb that's looking for little Bo-Peep.
For loaves, lemons, lettuce and lovely leek soup,
And a long-legged lad on the lawn with a hoop.
For lupins and lilac abloom in the lane,
And leaves on the laurel tree a-glisten with rain.

How many *words* beginning with L or l are in
this rhyme?

Answer: 22

36

Make no mistake!

M is for a moment and the months of March and May.

For milk and meat and margarine, and the money we must pay.

For mother making merry music as she mops and shakes the mat.

For mule and mole and monkey and a mouse who met a cat.

You may send a man a message or a magazine by post.

Make no mistake, you must have M for much and more and most!

How many *words* beginning with M or m are in this rhyme?

N is next!

N's for nice new neighbours living very near.
Their nephew's name is Nigel, their niece is Nell,
  I hear.
And N's for neck and nose and nails,
The news at nine, November gales.
A nightingale, a natterjack, a newt in a net;
And nettles, nuts and nests you should never forget.

How many *words* beginning with N or n are in
this rhyme?

Answer: 23

Oh dear!

O's for ostrich, owl or ox,
Old ornaments in an open box.
An outing in an omnibus,
An ocean of oysters or octopus.
Or orchards full of olive trees
And oodles of oranges from overseas.

How many *words* beginning with O or o are in this rhyme?

Answer: 20

39

Pick-a-P

P's for pool and a picnic in the park.
Pussies that purr and puppies that bark,
Ponies in paddocks, pink pigs in a sty,
Proud peacocks preen, plump pullets peck rye.
P's for plum pudding, a peach and a pear,
Popcorn and pancakes you toss in the air.

How many *words* beginning with P or p are in this rhyme?

Queue for Q

Q's for the questions you're asked in a quiz –
Where is Quebec, Queenstown and Cadiz?
For a quivering queue at a quarter to eight
Quarrelling because the quick bus is quite late.
For a quizzical queen in a quilted skirt
Watching Quentin play quoits – he's quite an
    expert.

How many *words* beginning with Q or q are in
this rhyme?

Answer: 16

Rd?

R's for a ride on a really rough road,
For rhubarb and raspberries by the load,
Ripe and ready to eat with a spoon,
In a rickety rickshaw in old Rangoon.
R is for rubies and roses red
For roach that rest on the river bed.

How many *words* beginning with R or r are in this rhyme?

Answer: 17

See S?

S is for sun that shines high up in the sky.
S is for a ship at sea sailing slowly by.
S is for my sister Sally skipping off to school,
S is for six sleepy sheep with coats of shaggy wool.
S is for a sneeze, a smile, a Saturday surprise –
Scarlet slippers, silver skates and stars in someone's
  eyes.

How many *words* beginning with S or s are in
this rhyme?

T Time!

T is for tick-tock and telling the time,
For tying things up with thread or with twine.
For a ticket to travel on the ten-thirty train
To the town terminus and back again.
T is for tiddler, tadpole, turtle and toad,
And the terrible tiger with two eyes that glowed.

How many *words* beginning with T or t are in
this rhyme?

Answer: 29

U can do it!

U is for umbrella, useful to keep us dry.
U is for an umpire, 'out,' you'll hear him cry.
Uncle wears a uniform, he's an unusual man.
Ursula can't understand, but Aunty Una can.
U's for Uganda and Uruguay, umpteen miles away,
Upset, upstairs and upside down are three more Us
   to say.

How many *words* beginning with U or u are in
this rhyme?

Variety

V is for the purple violet flowering in spring,
For a village in the valley and vines that climb and
    cling.
For vulture, vixen and for vole,
For volley ball and vaulting pole,
Vegetables, vitamins, vinegar too,
And a variety of Valentines sent to you.

How many *words* beginning with V or v are in
this rhyme?

Answer: 14

46

Work at it!

W is for wolf and weasel, a walrus and a wee white goat,
For a welcoming waiter wearing a wig and woolly waistcoat.
W's for winter weather, it's windy, wild and wet,
Wear Wellingtons and waterproofs and wet we will not get.
W's for a wonderful wizard in a tall and pointed hat,
And a wicked old witch who whispers weird spells to her wily cat.

How many *words* beginning with W or w are in this rhyme?

X-asperating

Words that begin with X are *ex*tremely few,
But X is for X-ray, an inside view of you.
A xylophone makes music – with a hammer you
   must strike it,
And X is for Xmas – spell it this way if you like it.
Have you met Xavier, the excitable cat?
And Xs are for kisses – did you know that?

How many *words* beginning with X or x are in
this rhyme?

Answer: 4

Y?

Y is for a young dog, you'll hear it yelp and yap.
For Yugoslavia, York and Yukon somewhere on
  your map.
Y is for a yacht and a yawl anchored in the bay,
Y is for a tired youth who's yawned since
  yesterday.
Y's for Yorkshire pudding, yoghurt and for yam,
And for a yellow egg yolk to eat with crispy ham.

How many *words* beginning with Y or y are in
this rhyme?

Zoo-m

Z's for zoo and zero, another word for nought.
Z is for the zither my Auntie Zoë bought.
Z is for the zest and zeal she plays it with each
    day.
And Z is for a zig-zag line zipping on its way.
Z is for a Zulu warrior, bravest in a fight.
Z is for zebra with stripes of black and white.

How many *words* beginning with Z or z are in
this rhyme?

Animals

**If you want to play some games,
Can you guess these creatures' names?**

1 It tunnels underneath the ground,
    And flicks long ears at every sound.
With whiskers long and nose a-twitch,
    You'll spot it hiding in the ditch.
Out it jumps – see its tail
    Bobbing over hill and dale.

2 It's fat and round and has a snout
    With which it pushes things about.
It lives on a farm – its house is a sty,
    It grunts at us when we pass by.
Coloured pink or black and white
    If it's tail is curly, it's all right!

Answers: 1 Rabbit, 2 Pig

3 Big as a house, lives in the sea,
  Not often seen by you and me.
No legs at all but a powerful tail,
  You couldn't keep it in a pail.
It squirts up water like a spout,
  A gigantic creature there is no doubt.

Answer: Whale

If you want to play some games,
Can you guess these creatures' names?

4   This one has no legs or fur,
       It does not squeak, it does not purr.
          It does have a tail that's coloured gold
       It likes the water running cold.
          It cannot fly, but it can swim,
       In a pond or a tank, filled to the brim!

5   Long and thin – lives underground.
          Moves around without a sound.
       Out it wriggles, which end is its head?
          Its colour is a brownish red.
       It has no arms, no legs, no feet,
          This is one we cannot eat!

6   Slithering, rippling, long and thin,
          Slithering round in a scaly skin.
       See it coil around a tree,
          Hope it keeps away from me!
       Rippling, slithering, twisting around,
          If angry, it makes a hissing sound.

Answers: **4** Goldfish, **5** Worm, **6** Snake

54

7 My memory's good – I never forget.
   My tusks and my trunk you'll never forget.

8 I am a man's best friend, I say.
   I will guard him night and day.

9 I'm as brave as brave can be.
   The king of the jungle they call me.

10 I am little with a coat of wool.
   One day I followed Mary to school.

11 I bray sometimes but I'll give you a ride,
   If you come and see me at the sunny seaside.

12 I give you milk and butter too
   I live on a farm and not in a zoo!

Answers: **7** Elephant, **8** Dog, **9** Lion, **10** Lamb, **11** Donkey, **12** Cow

13 One day I went to a party –
  What do you think was there?
They were sitting on the table –
  I really had a scare.
My friends all started laughing
  And said 'Oh – can't you see?
They're all made out of sugar –
  We're eating them for tea!'

14 My coat is smooth and silky fur,
  And when I'm pleased I always purr.

15 Peter lost his kite one day.
   Up it flew and then away.
The kite was happy flying free,
   Until it landed in a tree.
Peter looked up and said 'Oh dear,
   I'll never reach it there, I fear.'
Then over the wall appeared a head.
'What are you standing on?' young Peter said.
'Nothing, my friend – it's all just me.
   I'll reach your kite,' it said with glee.
'I've nice long legs and a long neck too,
   I really belong inside a zoo!'

Who reached Peter's kite?

Answer: 5 Giraffe

16 Tadpoles are always very small,
    A head and tail and that is all.
I like to watch them dart about
    When April sunshine brings them out.

But tadpoles grow as children do
    Just think and you will know it's true
One day you'll see upon a log
    Not your tadpole but a . . .

Answer: Frog

58

Colours

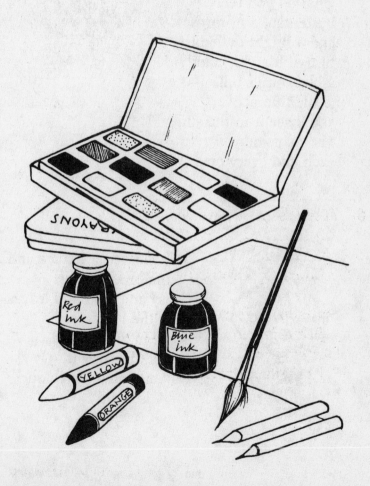

Lots of colour

1 Think of a colour –
   what can it be?
   Look all around you,
   what do you see?
   A buttercup, a primrose
   and a bright daffodil.
   A fluffy little chick and
   a blackbird's bill.
   And high up above,
   you'll see it in the sun,
   . . . is the colour of
   each and every one!

2 A cucumber, a lettuce and
   small round peas,
   Grass in a field and leaves
   on the trees.
   See it in an emerald,
   sparkling bright,
   Do you know the colour?
   . . . is right!

3 Think of a colour –
     what can it be?
Look all around you –
     what do you see?
A policeman's buttons
     and his whistle too.
The very best tea pot,
     spoons polished like new.
Tinsel and glitter
     on the Christmas tree
... is the colour
     that we can see.

4 A sky that is clear,
     a lake so still.
Forget-me-nots and bluebells
     growing on a hill.
Waves of the sea
     splashing all around
... is the colour
     that we have found.

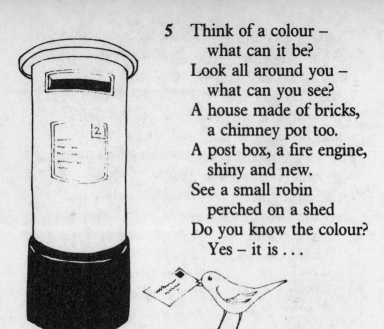

5 Think of a colour –
     what can it be?
Look all around you –
     what can you see?
A house made of bricks,
     a chimney pot too.
A post box, a fire engine,
     shiny and new.
See a small robin
     perched on a shed
Do you know the colour?
     Yes – it is . . .

6 A piglet's ears
     a piglet's nose
The petals on
     a pretty rose.
A little mouth
     waiting to be fed.
. . . is the colour —
     not quite red!

Answers: 5 Red, **6** Pink

62

7 This colour seems drab
and not very bright.
I wonder?
Do you think I'm right?
Think of chestnuts,
All glossy new,
Chocolate creams and a
polished shoe!
Chimney pots –
nice warm house.
A hooty owl and a
squeaky mouse.
Toffee apples,
a gingerbread man
And sausages sizzling
in the pan.

8 Think of scampering little mice
and donkeys that are always nice.
Enormous elephants in the zoo,
pigeons are this colour, too.

9 For special colours that I need,
　　I have a system that's guaranteed.
　With my brush I mix some blue,
　　Then I look for yellow too.
　Swirl them together round and round,
　　Now guess the colour that I have found!

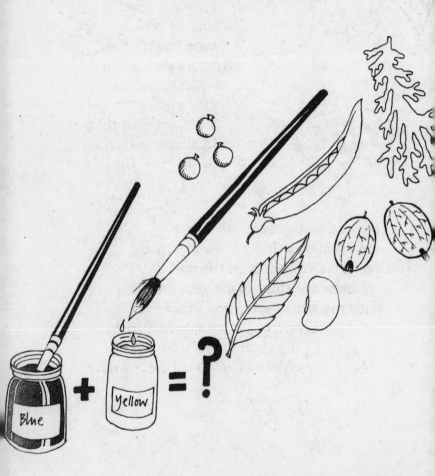

Answer: Green

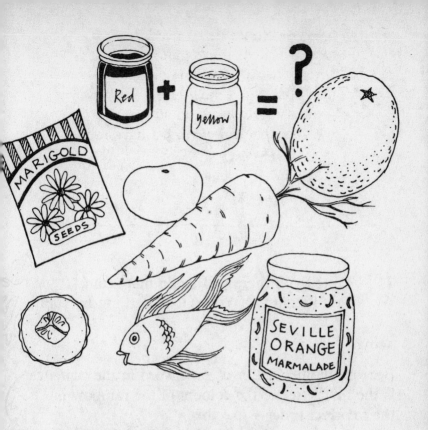

10 For special colours that I need
    I have a system that's guaranteed.
With my brush some red I mix
    And yellow too – it sounds like tricks.
Swirl them together, round and round,
    Now guess the colour that I have found!

Answer: Orange

11   To tell you there will be no more rain,
       Say 'Richard Of York Goes Battling In Vain.'

Why?

Because the first letter of each word in the sentence is the first letter of the colours of the rainbow in their correct order – like this:

I wonder? Can you tell me?
Do you really know?
   All the different colours in a bright rainbow?
First there's red and orange,
   Next comes yellow and green,
Blue, indigo and violet –
   All these can be seen.
So, when you see a rainbow
   That tells you,
'No more rain,'
   Say Richard Of York Goes Battling In Vain!

Fruit and Vegetables

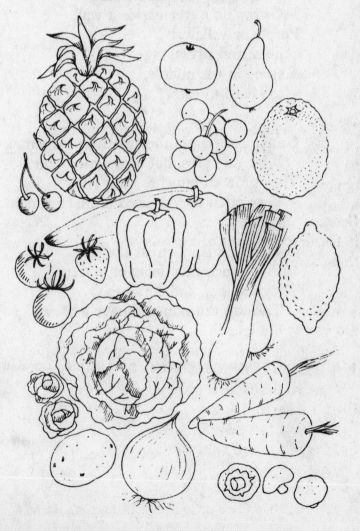

Why not try some pieces of fruit?
Must be something here to suit . . .

1   Not too large – not too small,
       Grows on a tree beside a wall.
    Purple or yellow,
       juicy and sweet,
    A stone in the middle,
       too hard to eat.

2   Green and purple they ripen in the sun,
       With tiny pips, but sometimes none.
    They grow in bunches on a vine,
       Very often they're used to make wine!

3   Grown in a land across the sea
       In a bunch they hang on a tree.
    They are long and curvy too,
       Take off the skin and have a chew!

Answers: 1 Plum, 2 Grapes, 3 Bananas

68

4 These are leaves we need not cook.
     You'll see them in a *Salads* book
And in the gardens and shops you pass,
     They're crisp and curly and green as grass.

5 Before you eat it – peel off its skin
     And throw it in the rubbish bin
It will divide into neat little bits
     Be careful now – you might find pips!

6 Grown in the garden or bought in a shop,
     Open their pods and hear them pop.
Inside they're round and hard and green.
     Cook – then balance on a fork when they're
       soft and green.

Answers: **4** Lettuce, **5** Orange, **6** Peas

7 This favourite fruit grows on a tree,
    Green, red and yellow ones you will see.
With a short dark stem and seeds inside,
    When you take a bite you must open wide.

8 Small and red and fruity
    Bite it and it's juicy
Make it into jam and spread
    It on a slice of bread.

9 It looks like a bulb with a papery skin
    Darker outside and white within.
When peeling it the smell's quite strong,
    Bringing tears to your eyes – but not for long.

Answers: 7 Apple, **8** Strawberry, **9** Onion

70

I Spy!

I spy something
   Beginning with C.
Lives on a farm
   And gives milk to you and me.

I spy two words
  Beginning with J,
High in the sky
  Flying on its way.

I spy someone
   Whose job begins with F,
He works on his farm
   And his name is Jeff!

I spy something
　　Beginning with D.
Off the lead in the park
　　It's running free.

Answer: Dog

I spy something
   Beginning with I.
It's an Eskimo's house
   That's what I spy!

I spy something
 Beginning with K
A small fluffy pet
 Who loves to play.

I spy someone
    Beginning with A.
She's my mum's sister
    Who has just come to stay!

I spy something
  Beginning with S.
It's always high above us
  I bet you can guess!

I spy something
    Beginning with B.
Spread on some butter and jam
    And eat it for tea!

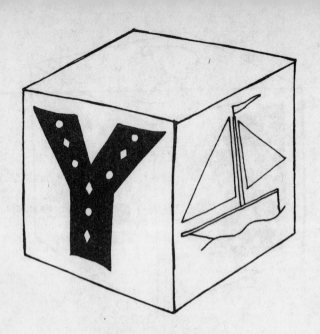

I spy something
    Beginning with Y.
It's inside the eggs
    We often buy.

I spy something
   Beginning with L.
A lick on a stick
   That sweetshop owners sell.

I spy something
  Beginning with O
Gallons of water
  Rolling to and fro.

Answer: Ocean

I spy something
  Beginning with Q.
It's a feather you could write with.
  Yes of course it's true.

I spy something
    Beginning with M
We need lots of this
    To buy a sparkling gem!

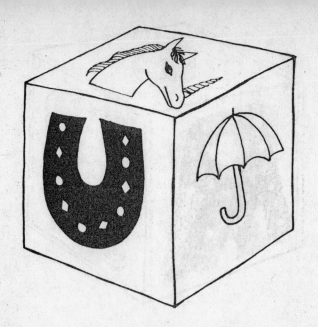

I spy someone
　　Beginning with U.
It's my father's brother –
　　Now you know who.

I spy something
    Beginning with R
It's a name for a dog
    And a make of car.

I spy something
   Beginning with V.
It throws out hot ashes
   And frightens me!

I spy people
   Beginning with N.
They live next door to me
   And I live next door to them!

People

People Poems

1   I see someone sail out on a cold, grey sea
    To catch fish in nets for you and for me.
    Tomorrow we'll cook some, they'll sizzle in the
        pan,
    And we will say 'thank you' to the brave . . .

Answer: Fisherman

2 I see someone – a welcome sight –
Making sure I'm feeling all right.
If I'm not well
She can tell,
For she is a ... who works at night.

3 I see someone who drives about all day.
He stops and starts for people and the people
    have to pay
  To travel with him into town.
  At quiet times they all sit down,
  At busy times they stand and sway.
'I am a ... ..,' he would say.

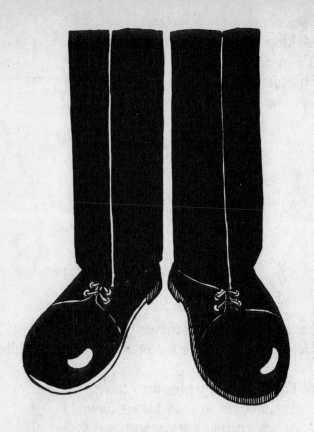

4 I see someone who works all day and night,
  Wearing a uniform with silver buttons bright.
Up and down the streets he goes
  Walking on his beat,
He's the friendly ...
  Whom we often meet.

Riddle-me-Rees

Think of a letter

1   The first letter is for sock and shoe
The second for uphill
The next is for the news that's new
The fourth for dig and drill.
The fifth begins an apple, an apricot an ape
And last of all start yesterday, yes, and yards of tape.

Put the letters all together and what do they say?
It's the first day of the week of course. And it is called . . .

2 Think of a letter – you'll find it in boat
In trousers and blouse – and also in coat
You'll find it in John and also in Joe.
That's right, you have guessed it
The letter is . . .

3 Think of a letter – you'll find in June
In Aunty and Uncles, in sun and in moon.
You'll find it in pencil and also in pen,
In now and in never –
The letter is . . .

4 Think of a letter – you'll find it in night
In cat and in kitten, in train and in kite.
You'll find it in star, and you'll find it in tree
You'll find it in tractor
Of course, it is . . .

5 The first letter's for mountain, for mouse and
   for more.
The second's for off and onion and oar.
The third is for nine and nothing as well,
The fourth is for daisy down in the dell.
Fifth is for anything any old time.
The last is for you and this is your rhyme.
Write down the letter and see what they say
Yes – that's right, you've guessed it, it spells
   out . . .

Shapes

Circles and squares are everywhere

1 Post on a fence and bars on a gate,
Lots of things are very ...
Electric wires and chimneys tall,
Walls of a house and pipes up the wall.
Four ... lines will make an E
Lots of ... things for you to see.

2 I see a . . . in the letter C,
The . . . of the moon, looking down at me.
The . . . of a bridge and the . . . of a hill,
The beautiful . . . of a pelican's bill.
A banana has a . . . that's for sure
Look all around and find some more.

3 What a lot of things a . . . makes,
Like ball and orange and wheel and cakes.
A china plate, a clock, the sun,
A top, a hoop, a currant bun.
Saucer, wedding ring, balloon,
A crown, an O and a big full moon.

4 Guess my shape is the name of this game,
All my sides are exactly the same.
Draw four lines and join each one,
See what shape it has become.
I'm sure that you must be aware
that you have drawn a perfect . . .

Sounds Like?

Think of a word

1 Think of a word
That sounds like snap.
Hot or cold water
Comes from a . . .

2 Think of a word
That sounds like jar.
And go for a ride
In a shiny . . .

3 Think of a word
That sounds like male.
When it's very windy
It's blowing a . . .

4 Think of a word
That sounds like again.
The water runs away
And down a . . .

Answers: 1 Tap, 2 Car, 3 Gale, 4 Drain

102

5 Think of a word
That sounds like rage.
It's a yellow canary
In a gilded . . .

6 Think of a word
That sounds like daft.
I float down the river
On a homemade . . .

7 Think of a word
That sounds like make.
Would you like
A nice cream . . .

8 Think of a word
That sounds like wall.
Towers and steeples
Are very . . .

WALL!

9 Think of a word
That sounds like land.
At the seaside we find
Water and . . .

10 Think of a word
That sounds like calm.
The middle of your hand
Is called the . . .

11 Think of a word
That sounds like lap.
A puppy's noise
Is called a . . .

12 Think of a word
That sounds like part.
I'd like to eat
A strawberry ...

13 Think of a word
That sounds like smash.
If you walk in a puddle
You make a ...

14 Think of a word
That sounds like fat.
On the top of your head
You wear a ...

15 Think of a word
That sounds like lawn.
When you're tired
You often . . .

16 Think of a word
That sounds like say.
If it's not night
It must be . . .

17 Think of a word
That sounds like need.
If it's not a flower
It could be a . . .

18 Think of a word
That sounds like bean.
If you're not dirty
You're probably . . .

Things with Wings

If you want to play some games,
Can you guess these creatures' names?

1 Buzzes here and buzzes there
    Hear it in the summer air.
Into a flower and out again,
    Gathering pollen grain by grain.
Back to the hive where honey sweet
Is made to give us a tea-time treat.

2 Black spots on a coat of red
    Tiny feelers on its head,
It hides among the leaves so green
    So small it hardly can be seen.
Pick it up and then you may
See tiny wings as it flies away.

3 This fine bird is very proud,
Its head is crested, its call is loud.
Although it has wings it seldom flies.
Watch it closely for a surprise –
In glorious colours its tail will spread,
Blue and green with a silver thread.

4 This bird sits on a perch and squawks
And sometimes too it even talks.
At other times you'll see it preen
Its feathers of blue, red or green.

5 See this creature flash about
   Darting in and darting out.
Over water, it hovers, then
   Spots its prey and darts again.

6 It's black and yellow, but not a bee;
   Stings you if it gets angry.
So be careful, don't go near;
Stay away – keep well clear.

7 It's up in the sky
   Flying very high
In the sun its wings shine bright
Then into cloud and it's out of sight.

8 Down under in Australia where it has its
   home
   Lives a bird that's very big and has never,
   ever flown.
   It has long, long legs and a long neck too,
   No, it's not an ostrich, it's called an . . .

9 On the farm you'll find it
   Pecking here and there.
   On the farm you'll hear it
   Clucking everywhere.
   And if you'd like an egg for tea,
   It may have laid one – look and see.

10 Quietly, quietly in the sky,
Not a sound as it glides by
It has no engine to make it go,
Air currents and wind help it fly, you know.
What is it?

11 We're very, very small,
Only some of us have wings
But we're busy little things
And hardly rest at all.

12 Tiny creatures – not often seen,
Wearing dresses of gossamer sheen.
Imagine them flying on fragile wings
And dancing about in magic rings.